Table of Contents

Chapter 1: The Great Homework Disaster

Max's Excuse: "The dog ate my math book!"
Excuse Rating: 7/10 – Convincing, but needed more evidence.

It was a quiet Sunday evening, the kind that should've been perfect for catching up on homework. But for Max Harrison, there was only one thing worse than math homework: actually doing it.

Max sat at his desk, his math book open to a page filled with intimidating equations. He tapped his pencil against his cheek, his eyes wandering to the window where Peanut, his golden retriever, lounged in the fading sunlight. Peanut had one ear flopped lazily over his face, completely unaware of the chaos brewing in Max's head.

"This is impossible," Max muttered, staring at the word algebra like it was written in ancient hieroglyphics. He closed the book with a dramatic sigh and flopped back in his chair. "I need a way out of this."

That's when it hit him. A story. A magnificent excuse that would get him off the hook. He glanced at Peanut, who yawned and stretched, oblivious to his newfound role in Max's master plan.

Five minutes later, Max burst into the kitchen, clutching his math book—or what was left of it. The pages were torn and wrinkled, and the corners had suspicious-looking bite marks.

"Mom! Dad!" Max cried, waving the destroyed book in the air. "Peanut ate my homework!"

His mom, who was stirring a pot of spaghetti sauce, raised an eyebrow. "Peanut did what now?"

Max held up the book for dramatic effect. "He got hungry, I guess. One minute I was working, and the next, chomp!" He imitated a vicious biting motion.

His dad looked over the top of his newspaper. "Peanut? The same dog who refuses to eat his kibble unless it has gravy on it?"

"Yes! That Peanut!"

Max insisted. "He's a wild animal when it comes to math books."

Peanut wandered into the kitchen at that exact moment, tail wagging, completely unaware of the accusations being hurled at him. He plopped down at Max's feet and started licking his paw.

"He doesn't look guilty to me," his mom said, eyeing the dog.

"Guilt is his strategy," Max said, crouching down to point at Peanut like a detective presenting evidence. "Look at that innocent face. It's all an act!"

His mom sighed. "Well, you'll have to explain this to Mrs. Greene tomorrow."

Max froze. Mrs. Greene, his math teacher, was not one to let things slide. She had a way of looking at you that made you confess to things you hadn't even done.

"Explain? Like... in person?" Max asked, his voice faltering.

"Unless you want me to call her and tell her the dog ate your homework," his mom replied, smirking.

Max gulped. This was going to take more effort than he thought.

The next morning, Max sat in math class, clutching his mutilated book. Peanut's teeth marks looked convincing enough, but Mrs. Greene wasn't one to be swayed by theatrics.

"Max, where's your completed homework?" she asked, scanning the room with her trademark eagle eyes.

"Um, about that..." Max held up the tattered book. "There was an incident. Peanut got to it before I could finish."

"Peanut?" Mrs. Greene raised an eyebrow.

"My dog," Max clarified, standing up and holding the book higher for everyone to see.

A few snickers erupted from the back of the classroom.

Mrs. Greene took the book from Max and examined it. "So, you're telling me that your dog chewed up your math homework?"

"Yes, ma'am," Max said confidently. "He's got a thing for geometry."

The class erupted in laughter, but Mrs. Greene wasn't amused. "Max, do you have any proof of this… 'incident'?"

Max hesitated. "Proof?"

"Yes," Mrs. Greene said, crossing her arms. "If your dog ate your homework, surely there's evidence—teeth marks, maybe even a photograph of the culprit in action?"

"Uh…" Max's mind raced. "Well, I didn't think to take a picture, but I have witnesses!"

"Witnesses?" Mrs. Greene's tone was skeptical.

"Yes! My mom, my dad—they both saw the devastation," Max said, trying to sound convincing. "And Peanut, of course. He's the prime suspect."

Mrs. Greene sighed and handed the book back to him. "Max, I'll give you until tomorrow to redo the assignment. But next time, I suggest you keep your math book out of Peanut's reach."

"Yes, ma'am," Max said, slumping into his chair.

That evening, Max sat at the dinner table, pushing peas around his plate. He'd gotten away with it—for now. But his parents weren't letting him off the hook so easily.

"Max," his dad said, folding his arms, "we need to talk about this Peanut ate my homework story."

"What about it?" Max asked, trying to sound innocent.

"You're telling me that Peanut, who hasn't chewed on anything since he was a puppy, suddenly decided to devour your math book?"

"Maybe he was bored?" Max offered weakly.

His mom chimed in. "Max, we know you didn't do your homework. Why not just admit it?"

Max sighed. "Because... I didn't want to get in trouble."

"Do you think you're not in trouble now?" his dad asked, raising an eyebrow.

"Not as much as I would've been," Max muttered.

His dad shook his head. "You can't keep making excuses, Max. Sooner or later, they're going to catch up with you."

Max didn't reply. He was already thinking about the next day—and the next excuse he might need.

As he lay in bed that night, staring at the ceiling, an idea began to form. If Mrs. Greene wanted proof, he'd give her proof. But this time, it wouldn't involve Peanut.

Max's eyes wandered to the mess of toys on his bedroom floor. His mom had been nagging him to clean it up for weeks, but tonight, it looked like an opportunity.

A sly grin spread across his face. "Aliens," he whispered to himself. "Nobody can argue with aliens."

Peanut, curled up at the foot of Max's bed, let out a sleepy huff as if to say, Here we go again.

Max rolled over, already crafting the perfect story for tomorrow. Little did he know, this excuse was about to take his imagination—and his consequences—to a whole new level.

Chapter 2: Alien Invasion

Max's Excuse: "Aliens rearranged my room!"
Excuse Rating: 6/10 – Sparkly footprints were a nice touch.

Max stared at the chaos in his room and crossed his arms. His mom had been clear: Clean your room, Max, or you're grounded for a week. But this? This wasn't just untidiness—this was sabotage.

Peanut tilted his head from his spot by the door, tail wagging. Max gave the golden retriever a warning look. "Don't even think about it, Peanut. I know better than to blame you twice."

Then it hit him: Aliens.

He gasped dramatically, stepping over the toppled action figures. "Of course! This isn't my mess—it's an alien invasion!"

The story formed in his head as he examined the scene. His spaceship model was cracked open, clearly evidence of extraterrestrial tampering. The spilled cereal? Obviously, aliens trying to decode Earth food. The socks? Surely part of some top-secret intergalactic experiment.

"Lila!" he yelled, running out of the room.

His eight-year-old sister was in the living room, coloring a picture of a unicorn. She looked up, annoyed. "What do you want, Max?"

"You need to help me," Max declared. "Aliens invaded my room last night and made a total mess!"

Lila blinked. "Aliens? Really?"

"Yes! They left footprints and everything." He grabbed her hand, pulling her toward his room.

When she saw the disaster, she squinted. "It just looks like your room is... normal messy."

Max gasped in mock horror. "That's what they want you to think! But look at the cereal bowl—it's been moved! And my action figures—they've been strategically knocked over!"

Lila folded her arms. "What's in it for me if I help you?"

Max rolled his eyes. "Uh, saving the planet from alien spies?"

She raised an eyebrow, unimpressed.

"Fine. I'll let you play with my drone for a whole week."

"Deal."

Max immediately got to work spinning the most elaborate story he could. With Lila's reluctant cooperation, they planted "alien footprints" made from a mix of flour and water leading from the window to the desk. Max even tipped over his trash can for added effect. By the time they were done, Lila stood back and surveyed the scene. "Okay, now what?"

"Now," Max said, grinning, "we show Mom the evidence."

"Aliens? Really?"

Mom stared at the chaos in Max's room, her hands on her hips. Max nodded enthusiastically. "I swear, Mom, I woke up, and it was like this! Look at the footprints! The aliens must have climbed through the window!"

Mom crouched down, inspecting the floury smudges. Lila stood behind Max, trying her best to look serious, though her lips twitched.

"You expect me to believe that little green men messed up your room because... why exactly?"

Max opened his mouth, then closed it. He hadn't thought that far ahead. "Um, research?"

Mom sighed. "Max, this looks suspiciously like you didn't want to clean your room and decided to cook up another one of your stories."

"But Mom, it's true!"

Mom stood up and pointed at the broom in the corner. "Clean this up, and no screen time until your room is spotless. Lila, you're off the hook— go play."

As Lila bolted, Max groaned. "This is so unfair. I'm telling you, aliens did this!"

"Max, if I see one more ridiculous excuse, you're grounded for real," Mom said firmly before leaving.

That night, Max lay in bed, staring at the ceiling. He felt the first hint of doubt. Maybe his alien excuse was a little over the top.

His thoughts were interrupted by a tapping sound at his window. He froze. Was it...?

Creeping to the window, he peeked outside. A branch swayed in the wind, brushing against the glass.

Max sighed. Aliens, huh? Maybe I should give the excuses a break.

Chapter 3: The Hamster Heist

Max's Excuse: "Gizmo stole my science project!"
Excuse Rating: 5/10 – Creative, but too many accomplices.

Max sat frozen at his desk as Mrs. Greene called on another student to present their science project. He barely heard the explanations about volcano models and ecosystem dioramas—his mind was racing. What am I going to say?

When Mrs. Greene called his name, Max stood hesitantly, clutching an empty folder. He shuffled to the front of the class, glancing at the cage where Gizmo, the class hamster, was nibbling on a sunflower seed.

"Where's your project, Max?" Mrs. Greene asked, her voice patient but firm.

Max hesitated for a moment before blurting out, "It's gone... because Gizmo stole it!"

The room went silent for half a second before laughter erupted. His best friend, Leo, smirked and leaned over to whisper loudly, "Great one, Max!"

Mrs. Greene raised an eyebrow, clearly unimpressed. "You're telling me that a hamster stole your solar system model?"

Max nodded vigorously, his confidence building despite the snickers. "Yes! I left it on my desk in the garage last night, and when I woke up, it was gone. I think Gizmo escaped, dragged it out through the window, and... and... chewed it up!"

"Gizmo chewed your science project," Mrs. Greene repeated flatly, crossing her arms.

"Yes! Hamsters have super strong teeth!" Max exclaimed.

"That's true," chimed in Mia, the class know-it-all. "Hamsters' teeth never stop growing. They're, like, ridiculously powerful for their size."

"Exactly!" Max seized on her comment, spinning his tale further. "Gizmo must have chewed through the bars, carried the model out piece by piece, and hid it somewhere. Probably in his secret hamster lair!"

Mrs. Greene sighed deeply. "Max, it's one thing to forget your project. It's another to blame the class hamster."

"But it's true!" Max insisted. He pointed at the cage dramatically. "Just check his cage! I bet there's glitter from the planets in there!"

The class erupted in laughter again.

At lunch, Max's story took on a life of its own.

Leo sat across from him in the cafeteria, munching on a sandwich. "So, Gizmo's like a little furry supervillain now? What's his evil plan—world domination?"

"Probably," Max said, leaning into the joke. "He's starting with the solar system. First my project, then the real planets!"

His friend Zara chimed in, giggling. "You should write a book about it: Gizmo the Galactic Hamster."

"I'd totally read that," said Ethan, who was sketching a hamster wearing a cape on his napkin.

Max grinned, feeling a strange mix of pride and guilt. The story was making him the center of attention, but deep down, he knew he was digging himself into a deeper hole.

By the time the bell rang for dismissal, Max's tale had grown into a full-fledged legend. Several classmates crowded around Gizmo's cage, peering in as if the hamster might reveal some incriminating evidence.

"Look at his cheeks!" Leo exclaimed. "What's he hiding in there?"

"Probably Jupiter," Ethan quipped, holding up his napkin sketch.

Max chuckled nervously. "Yeah, well... maybe he's planning his next heist."

Mrs. Greene wasn't laughing. She called Max over to her desk as the other students filed out of the classroom.

"Max, we need to have a serious conversation about honesty," she said.

Max gulped. "I am being honest! Gizmo—"

Mrs. Greene held up a hand. "Max, I don't know why you didn't bring your project, but blaming a defenseless hamster isn't the answer. I'll be calling your parents to discuss this."

Max's heart sank.

That evening, Max sat on his bed, staring at the half-finished solar system model in the corner of the garage. Peanut lay at his feet, wagging his tail lazily.

"Why do I keep doing this?" Max muttered to himself. Peanut tilted his head as if in response.

Max sighed. The truth was, it was easier to make up stories than to admit when he messed up. But now, his stories were starting to cause real problems.

Just then, his mom poked her head into his room. "Max, Mrs. Greene called. Care to explain why she thinks Gizmo is a tiny criminal mastermind?"

Max groaned. "It's... complicated."

"Well, you've got all night to work on that explanation—and to finish your science project," she said, setting a timer on his desk. "No dinner until it's done."Max watched her leave and slumped in his chair.

No more stories, he promised himself.

Chapter 4: The Case of the Missing Cupcakes

Max's Excuse: "The cupcakes vanished into a black hole!"
Excuse Rating: 8/10 – Bold, but the crumbs gave it away.

The smell of freshly baked cupcakes wafted through the house, teasing Max's senses as he lounged on the couch. He peeked into the kitchen, where his mom was carefully pulling the last tray from the oven. Golden cupcakes sat in perfect rows, their tops domed just right.

"Wow, Mom. Those look amazing," Max said, sidling closer.

"They're for the school bake sale," she replied, setting the tray on the counter. "Do not touch them. I'm heading to the store for frosting supplies. Tommy's upstairs if you need anything."

Max nodded, but his gaze lingered on the cupcakes. They seemed to glow under the kitchen light, whispering, Just one won't hurt.

As soon as the front door closed, Max crept into the kitchen. He inhaled deeply, imagining how they'd taste. "One cupcake won't even be missed," he muttered.

He reached for one, then stopped. What if Mom counts them? But the temptation was too strong. Carefully, he peeled the wrapper off a cupcake, popped it into his mouth, and chewed blissfully.

"Perfect," he mumbled, crumbs scattering onto his shirt.

One turned into two. Two turned into three. By the time he stopped, the tray was empty.

Max stared at the crumbs on the counter, his stomach sinking. "Oh no. What did I do?"

Footsteps thundered down the stairs, and his younger brother, Tommy, burst into the kitchen. "What smells so good?"

Max panicked. "Nothing! I mean, cupcakes. But you can't have any because—because a... cupcake black hole sucked them up!"

Tommy blinked. "What?"

"Yeah, it's a scientific phenomenon. Unstable kitchen particles form a vortex and—poof! Food disappears." Max gestured dramatically, hoping his brother would buy the story.

Tommy squinted at the empty tray. "Looks more like you ate them."

Max wiped at the crumbs on his shirt. "Pfft, no way! I'm the one trying to solve the mystery here."

"Uh-huh." Tommy crossed his arms. "Good luck explaining that to Mom."

Max groaned.

By the time his mom returned, Max had come up with a plan—or what he thought was a plan.

He sprinkled flour on the counter and tossed a few cupcake wrappers onto the floor. When his mom walked into the kitchen, he pointed and exclaimed, "Look! Evidence of a... a cupcake black hole!" Her eyes narrowed. "Max. Where are the cupcakes?"

"I told you! The black hole! It—"

She cut him off, raising the empty tray. "Then what's this?"

Max stammered, "Uh, well, the black hole closed after it... ate them all. But it definitely wasn't me."

"And the crumbs on your shirt?"

"Uh... fallout from the vortex?"

"Max!" she snapped, her voice sharp. "Enough. Did you eat the cupcakes?"

Max hesitated, his heart pounding. He glanced at Tommy, who stood in the doorway smirking. "It was Tommy!" Max blurted.

"What?" Tommy shouted.

"Yeah! He came downstairs and couldn't stop himself. I tried to stop him, but he just—he wouldn't listen!" Max said, layering on the fake distress.

Tommy looked like he might explode. "I didn't even know there were cupcakes until I smelled them!

And you have crumbs all over you, genius!"

Max's mom folded her arms. "Well, Max?"

Realizing his story was falling apart, Max played his final card. "Maybe Peanut ate them?" he suggested weakly, glancing at their golden retriever, who lay snoring on the floor.

His mom raised an eyebrow. "Peanut? Who hasn't moved in the last hour?"

"Yes! He might've done it while we weren't looking. He's sneaky like that!"

Tommy groaned. "Mom, can we just ground him already? He's obviously lying."

Max's mom sighed deeply. "Max, I've told you before that honesty is the best policy. Why didn't you just tell the truth?"

Max shuffled his feet. "I... I didn't want you to be mad."

"I'm not mad about the cupcakes, Max. I'm upset that you're lying to cover it up. When you lie, it makes it harder for people to trust you."

Max looked down at Peanut, whose wagging tail seemed to say, *You're on your own, buddy.* "Okay, fine," Max muttered. "I ate them. All of them."

His mom sighed again, but this time it sounded more tired than angry. "Thank you for telling the truth. But you'll be baking a new batch—and cleaning the kitchen. Got it?"

Max nodded. "Got it."

"And you're grounded. No video games this weekend."

"But—"

"No buts." She handed him an apron.

As Max scrubbed the counter, he glanced at Tommy. "You didn't have to rat me out, you know."

Tommy smirked. "You ratted yourself out, cupcake genius."

Chapter 5: The Case of the Missing Cupcakes

Max's Excuse: "The cupcakes vanished into a black hole!"
Excuse Rating: 8/10 – Bold, but the crumbs gave it away.

Max stared at the piece of paper in front of him—his report card. It was terrible. Every subject was marked with a big, red "C" or lower. The notes from his teachers were even worse. "Needs improvement," "Missed several assignments," and the worst one of all, "Shows potential but lacks effort." The words seemed to mock him, a reminder of all the excuses he'd made, and how they'd come back to bite him.

He could already hear his mom's voice in his head: "Max, what happened to your grades this term? You promised you'd do better." The disappointment in her tone would be unbearable. There was no way he could let her see this report card.

That's when it hit him—the perfect excuse.

"Peanut," Max said, his voice quiet but determined. His golden retriever, Peanut, was lying on the floor, wagging his tail lazily. Max stared at him, an idea forming. Peanut always looked so innocent, so adorable. How could anyone blame him for anything?

"Peanut must've eaten it!" Max thought out loud. He jumped up, holding the report card in his hand. "Mom! You're not going to believe this, but Peanut ate my report card!"

His heart pounded as he made his way to the living room, where his mom was sitting on the couch, reading a book. He waved the crumpled report card in front of her face. "Mom, you won't believe it—Peanut ate my report card!"

His mom raised an eyebrow. "What are you talking about, Max?"

"I'm serious!" Max said, walking over to the couch and plopping down next to her. "It was laying on the table, and then I turned around, and Peanut—well, Peanut got it!"

Max's mom didn't say anything for a long moment, just staring at him with a raised eyebrow. Then, she sighed. "Max, you're not fooling anyone."

Max blinked. "What do you mean? Peanut really did eat it!"

"Max," his mom said, putting down her book. "Peanut is a dog. He doesn't eat paper. He's not some sort of paper-eating monster. And if he did, I'd expect there to be some, you know, teeth marks, or bits of it around the house. But look around. There's nothing. No paper. No mess."

Max's face turned bright red, but he wasn't going to back down.

"Well... he must've eaten it all," Max stammered, his fingers tightening around the edges of the report card.

His mom shook her head, her face softening with a sigh. "Max, you know I'm not angry. But I am disappointed. We've talked about this before. You promised to do better. What happened?"

Max looked at the report card again, feeling the weight of his mom's words. His fingers traced the red marks on the paper. He knew the truth. He hadn't tried his best. He'd put things off, made excuses, and hoped it would all just work itself out. But it didn't. And now, here he was, blaming his dog.

"Mom," Max said quietly, his voice almost a whisper. "I'm really sorry. I didn't... I didn't do my best. I should've studied harder. I should've paid attention more in class."

His mom smiled at him, a knowing look in her eyes. "I'm glad you're finally being honest, Max. You know what you need to do next, right?"

Max nodded. "Yeah... work harder."

She patted him on the shoulder. "That's right. But next time, don't blame Peanut. He's an innocent dog.

And I think we both know he didn't eat your report card."

Max chuckled nervously, rubbing the back of his neck. "Right. I got carried away."

Just then, Peanut walked over, tail wagging, and plopped down on Max's feet. Max looked down at the dog, who gave him a look of pure innocence. How could he have blamed him for all of this? He couldn't even imagine how Peanut would've chewed up a report card in the first place. The dog could barely even chew through a shoe.

"Alright, Peanut," Max said, scratching his dog behind the ears. "I promise I won't blame you next time."

As Max sat there, staring at the crumpled report card in his hands, he realized something important. The excuses he'd been making weren't helping anyone. They were only making things worse.

A sudden thought hit him—he needed to fix this. Not just his report card, but his entire approach to life. It was time to be more honest, more responsible. He wasn't going to let his lies take control anymore.

"Mom," he said, his voice firm. "I'm going to start studying harder. No more excuses. I mean it."

His mom smiled again, and this time it was a proud smile. "I'm glad to hear that, Max. I know you can do better. Just remember, honesty is always the best way to go."

Max nodded, feeling a sense of determination wash over him. It wasn't going to be easy, but he was ready to change. He was ready to stop lying and start taking responsibility for his actions.

The rest of the evening passed by in a blur. Max didn't feel like making excuses anymore. He spent some time with Peanut, doing his best to show him how sorry he was for dragging him into the mess. Later, Max even cracked open a textbook, determined to do better next time.

But as the night wore on, Max realized one thing: his mom was right. Lying had only made things worse. And he had learned the hard way that it was time to stop blaming others, especially Peanut, for his own mistakes.

Chapter 6: Operation Pizza Night

Max's Excuse: "Too sick to help... but pizza cures everything!"
Excuse Rating: 3/10 – My friends weren't buying it.

Max had always looked forward to pizza night—it was the highlight of his week. The warm, cheesy slices, the toppings galore, and the laughter of his family around the table. It was perfect... unless you were Max, and you had a perfectly good excuse for not lifting a finger to help.

"I think I'm coming down with something," Max said, dramatically clutching his stomach as he collapsed onto the couch. "I don't know if I can help tonight. I feel like I've got a fever, maybe the flu." He exaggerated a cough for effect.

His sister, Lila, rolled her eyes from across the room. "Max, you're fine," she said, not even bothering to look up from her tablet.

But Max wasn't going to let that stop him. This was the perfect opportunity to avoid the dreaded pizza-making chores. He could already hear his parents in the kitchen, chopping vegetables, spreading sauce, and doing the hard work. Max just had to stay in his sick act long enough to escape responsibility.

A few minutes later, his mom poked her head into the living room. "Max, can you help set the table?"

Max grimaced, sinking deeper into the couch. "I really don't think I can. I'm really not feeling well, Mom."

His mom gave him a skeptical look. "You don't look sick."

"Uh, I feel terrible," Max said, a little too quickly. "I need to lie down. I think I have a fever."

"Uh-huh. Okay, Max." She turned to go back to the kitchen, but then stopped and looked back at him. "If you're really sick, I'll get you some soup. But if you're faking, I'm going to make you help clean up after dinner."

Max's heart raced. He couldn't let her catch on. "I promise, Mom, I'm not faking. I'm just... really tired. I'll be okay."

With a sigh, his mom walked away, leaving Max alone with his lie. He felt a bit guilty, but it was worth it. He was sure he could get away with it.

But just as he settled back into the couch, there was a loud knock on the door. Max froze. Who could that be?

He opened the door to find his friends, Jack and Emma, standing on the porch, holding pizza boxes. "We brought pizza!" Jack grinned.

"We heard it was pizza night and thought we'd join you."

Max's stomach dropped. He couldn't just keep pretending to be sick now, not when they were standing right in front of him, with pizza in hand. He hadn't planned for this.

"Uh, hey guys..." Max stammered, trying to hide his panic. "I was just... lying down. I'm really not feeling great, you know?"

Jack raised an eyebrow, looking Max up and down. "You look fine to me. If you're not feeling well, why don't you just help with the pizzas?"

Max quickly waved his hand, attempting to brush it off. "I'm not feeling that bad. But, uh, you can go ahead and sit down. I'll, um... I'll just rest here."

Emma, who had always been the most observant of the group, narrowed her eyes. "Wait a minute," she said, crossing her arms. "Aren't you supposed to be setting the table, or something?"

Max's mouth went dry. "I... I thought I'd just... stay here and... rest. You guys can have the pizza, though. It's really good, I'm sure."

Emma and Jack exchanged a look, then both sat down at the table, where Max's mom was already spreading the toppings on the dough.

They didn't say anything right away, but Max could feel them staring at him, questioning his excuse.

Max tried to focus on the pizza. It was delicious, and the cheese stretched out perfectly with every slice. But he couldn't ignore the feeling that his friends weren't buying his sick act.

After a few moments of awkward silence, Jack finally broke it. "So, you're sick, huh? But you're still eating pizza?"

Max choked on his slice. "I mean... I'm just... really hungry," he said, his voice cracking. "Being sick doesn't mean I can't eat, right?"

Emma laughed lightly. "Yeah, right. You're sick, but you still managed to grab a slice before us. You sure you're not just avoiding chores?"

Max didn't answer immediately. His stomach turned, and his face flushed with guilt. He'd been caught. His lie wasn't fooling anyone.

His mom, who had been listening to the conversation from the kitchen, walked over with a knowing look. "Max," she said gently, "you don't have to fake being sick. We're a team here, and I'd rather you just help out than make up excuses."

Max swallowed, his head hanging in shame. "I'm sorry, Mom. I didn't mean to... I just didn't want to do the chores."

"Next time, just ask," his mom said with a smile. "We can all work together. No need to fake being sick."

Max nodded, feeling the weight of the lie lift off his shoulders. He had been so focused on avoiding the work that he hadn't thought about how it might affect the people around him. Jack and Emma weren't mad at him, but they were clearly starting to question his pattern of excuses.

The rest of the dinner was spent laughing and joking, with Max occasionally glancing at his friends, who kept throwing him teasing looks. It was clear that they didn't buy his excuse, and Max realized that his friends were starting to see through his habit of making up stories. They didn't mind helping out, but they didn't like being lied to.

As the evening wore on, Max realized something important: it wasn't just about avoiding chores, or dodging responsibility—it was about being honest. His friends were smart, and they could tell when he wasn't being truthful.

And though they were still his friends, Max could tell they were starting to question his honesty. When dinner was over, Max helped clean up, though he didn't feel like it. He knew he deserved the extra work after his antics. But as he washed the dishes and put the leftovers away, he couldn't help but think about what was coming next. He had to be more honest. It wasn't just about pizza night; it was about the kind of friend he wanted to be.

Chapter 7: The Big Bike Race Blunder

Max's Excuse: "Someone sabotaged my bike!"
Excuse Rating: 6/10 – Plausible, but no evidence.

Max had been dreaming about the neighborhood bike race for weeks. He'd seen the posters around town, the buzz in the school hallways, and the excitement in the eyes of his friends. This year, he was determined to win—no more second place. No more excuses.

At least, that's what he told himself.

The day of the race arrived, and Max felt confident—at first. The sun was shining, the air was crisp, and the roads were clear. His friends Jack and Emma were already warming up by the starting line, chatting and stretching, and Max was doing the same... sort of. He was adjusting his helmet and trying to make his bike look like it was in prime condition, even though he hadn't actually checked it in weeks.

"Ready to lose, Max?" Jack teased, his bike gleaming in the sunlight.

"I'm not losing this time," Max shot back, trying to sound more confident than he felt.

The race began with a loud whistle, and the group took off. Max pushed hard, pedaling faster than he'd ever pedaled before. But after just a few minutes, something didn't feel right.

His bike seemed sluggish, like it was dragging. Maxtried to ignore it, focusing on the road ahead, but every time he pushed down on the pedals, the bike felt slower and slower.

By the time they reached the first turn, Max was already trailing behind. Jack and Emma were a blur in front of him, their bikes zooming down the street. Max pushed harder, but it didn't help. He could hear his friends laughing and calling out to him from ahead, but all he could do was grit his teeth and keep pedaling.

It was no use. When they hit the final stretch, Max was far behind. His legs burned, his arms ached, and he could see his friends already crossing the finish line, their bikes skidding to a stop.

Max rolled across the finish line last, out of breath and thoroughly defeated. He looked around, hoping no one would notice how badly he'd lost.

But of course, they did.

Jack and Emma were already standing by the finish line, laughing and high-fiving each other. "You okay, Max?" Emma called, raising an eyebrow.

Max pulled his bike over to the side, pretending to be out of breath.

He put a hand on his side, hunching over to make it look like he was in pain. "Ugh... I think my bike was sabotaged," he said, grimacing.

"Sabataged?" Jack repeated, raising an eyebrow. "What do you mean?"

Max straightened up slightly, trying to look serious. "Yeah. Someone messed with my tires or something. It wasn't just me. It was definitely the bike."

Emma narrowed her eyes. "Max, come on. You were fine at the start. Maybe it's just that you didn't train enough."

Max shook his head. "No way. It was sabotage. I know it."

Jack and Emma exchanged a look. It was clear they didn't buy his excuse. But Max wasn't about to give up.

"I think it's the brakes, too," he said, inspecting his bike. "I couldn't even get them to work right! Someone must have—"

"Max," Emma interrupted, crossing her arms. "We saw you last week. You were riding fine. You didn't even bother checking your bike before the race. If anything, it was your lack of preparation that got you behind, not sabotage."

Max's face flushed. He opened his mouth to argue, but no words came out. Emma was right, of course. He hadn't checked his bike. He hadn't practiced as much as he'd said he did. But he wasn't ready to admit that yet. Not in front of his friends.

Jack put a hand on Max's shoulder, trying to lighten the mood. "Hey, it's just a race. You'll do better next time."

But Max couldn't shake the feeling of disappointment. He had been so sure he was going to win. Now, instead of owning up to his failure, he was making up stories to cover it up.

"Yeah, next time..." Max mumbled, feeling embarrassed.

They all headed back to their houses, but Max was too distracted by his thoughts to enjoy the ride home. He knew what he'd done. He'd blamed the bike, he'd lied about sabotage, and he had tried to hide the truth from his friends. But all it had done was make him look worse.

By the time Max got home, he could hear his parents talking in the kitchen. He put his bike in the garage and walked slowly inside, avoiding eye contact with his mom, who was preparing dinner.

"How was the race, Max?" she asked, wiping her hands on a dish towel.

Max hesitated, then shrugged. "I lost."

His mom smiled. "That's okay, sweetie. You can't win every time. It's about trying your best."

Max wasn't sure how to respond. He had tried, but he hadn't really prepared. And now, he had lied about the whole thing.

"Did you have fun, at least?" his mom asked, her tone casual.

"Yeah, but..." Max hesitated. He couldn't keep pretending anymore. "I didn't really train like I said I would. And I blamed my bike. But it wasn't really the bike. It was me."

His mom raised an eyebrow, clearly surprised. "It's good that you're being honest, Max. Sometimes it's hard to admit when we've made a mistake, but that's how we learn."

Max nodded, feeling the weight of his words. He wasn't proud of what he'd done, but at least he was being honest now.

That evening, when he was sitting in his room, Max thought about the race. He could have come clean about losing, but instead, he'd tried to cover it up with an excuse.

And now, he was left feeling like a failure, not because he lost, but because he couldn't be honest about it.

As he lay down in bed that night, Max made a promise to himself. The next time something went wrong, he would tell the truth, no matter how embarrassing it might be. Because the truth, he realized, was always easier to deal with than a lie.

Chapter 8: The Soggy Sock Scandal

Max's Excuse: "A frog broke the washing machine!"
Excuse Rating: 7/10 – Points for originality.

Max had always been quick with excuses, but today, he was going to take things to the next level.

It all started innocently enough. Max's mom asked him to help with the laundry. "Max, can you take these clothes out of the wash? And please fold them when you're done?"

Max, who had been planning to spend the afternoon playing his favorite video game, groaned in response. He had no interest in laundry. But as he trudged toward the laundry room, something caught his eye: a pair of wet, soggy socks sitting in the middle of the laundry basket.

"Ugh, what happened here?" Max muttered under his breath. The socks were completely drenched, and the washing machine was making a strange whirring noise.

He knew he had to come up with something—anything—to avoid taking responsibility for this. So, like a pro, Max began to formulate a plan. His sister, Lila, was walking down the hallway toward the kitchen, and Max saw his opportunity. He held up the soggy socks dramatically, hoping his performance would distract from the truth.

"Mom, something's wrong with the washing machine!

It's broken, and I think it flooded the laundry room!" Max called out.

His mom came rushing in. "Max, what are you talking about? The washing machine's been working just fine—"

"No, Mom, I'm serious! It was like a waterfall in there! And then, a frog jumped out of the machine and landed on the floor! It was huge! I'm telling you, there's a frog in the laundry room!"

His mom stopped mid-sentence, eyes widening with disbelief. "A frog? Max, there is no frog in the laundry room."

Max quickly jumped in, trying to salvage the situation. "Yeah, well, I thought maybe it was just hopping around, but it must have gone back into the pipes or something." He pointed dramatically toward the corner of the room. "Look, you can see where it splashed!"

Lila, who had been listening from the doorway, raised an eyebrow. "A frog? Really, Max?"

Max froze, realizing he had just added a ridiculous detail to his already-faulty excuse. Lila was eyeing him suspiciously now, and he knew that if anyone was going to figure out his lie, it would be her.

"I... I mean... yeah, I guess it could have been something else," Max stammered. "Like, I don't know... maybe a raccoon?" he added, trying to make the story seem a little more plausible.

His sister didn't buy it for a second. She crossed her arms and smirked. "A raccoon? In the laundry room?"

Max quickly changed the subject. "Anyway, it's not my fault! The machine's broken, and I was just trying to do the laundry like you asked. Maybe we should call a plumber or something."

At this point, Max's mom was starting to look concerned, but not for the reasons Max had hoped. "Max, I don't know what's going on here, but it's not a raccoon, and it's definitely not a frog. I'll be calling the repairman tomorrow."

Max's heart sank. He knew he wasn't getting out of this one. But rather than owning up to his mistake, he doubled down. He continued to spin his story, despite knowing it wasn't going to work.

"I promise, the washing machine is haunted or something," Max said, his voice full of false confidence. "It was a spooky laundry disaster.

Like, maybe the washing machine's got magic powers or something."

Lila was no longer paying attention. She had wandered over to the laundry room door and was fiddling with the handle. "Max," she said, in that tone that made him realize she was onto him, "did you forget to drain the washing machine after you put in the socks?"

Max's stomach twisted. His sister was way too sharp for her own good.

"No... I mean, yes! I forgot!" Max admitted, feeling cornered. "I forgot to drain it, okay? And the socks got stuck in there, and then they got wet. But the frog thing... that was real! It was real, I swear!"

Lila raised her eyebrows. "Max, you need to stop lying. You could have just told Mom you made a mistake. It would have been way easier than blaming it on a frog or a raccoon."

Max felt his face flush with embarrassment. He realized that Lila was right. The truth would have been far simpler—and less ridiculous—than the web of lies he'd created. Instead of just admitting that he'd forgotten to drain the machine properly, he'd let his imagination run wild and made things ten times worse.

His mom, now fully understanding the situation, shook her head with a smile. "Max, you really need to be more honest. It's okay to make mistakes, but it's not okay to blame everyone and everything else but yourself. You're going to have to clean up the laundry and apologize to Lila for lying."

Max groaned, feeling the weight of his actions. He had spent so much time trying to cover up a small mistake, but now he was in even more trouble than if he had just come clean from the start.

As he knelt down to clean up the laundry room, Max couldn't help but think about all the times he had used excuses in the past. Whether it was a missing homework assignment or a broken bike, he had always tried to shift the blame. But today, he realized that the truth—no matter how small or embarrassing—was always the better choice.

With a sigh, Max took a deep breath and finally admitted, "Okay, fine. I messed up. No frog. No raccoon. Just me not checking the machine properly."

Lila smiled, giving him a quick thumbs-up. "That wasn't so hard, was it?"

Max grinned sheepishly. "Nope. It wasn't. I guess I'll try to be more honest next time."

Chapter 9: The Bizarre Birthday Gift

Max's Excuse: "It's a rare collector's set!"
Excuse Rating: 5/10 – Too weird to be
believable.

Max stared at the calendar, his heart sinking into his stomach. It was Jack's birthday. His best friend. And yet, he had completely forgotten to get him a present. The party was later that afternoon, and Max had zero ideas on what to get Jack. It wasn't like he had forgotten the date—he had just been too distracted with other things. Now, as he sat at his desk, he felt a wave of panic creeping up on him.

"Think, Max, think!" he muttered to himself, staring at his cluttered room. His eyes darted over random objects—an old, half-used notebook, a few action figures, a stack of magazines—and then it hit him.

Jack loved collecting things. It wasn't a lot, but he did have a small collection of baseball cards, comic books, and action figures. Maybe Max could pull something together from his old stash. He started digging through his drawers. After a few minutes of rummaging, Max found a few mismatched action figures, an old comic book that Jack had lent him once, and a baseball cap that didn't even fit him anymore.

Perfect. He grabbed a gift bag and shoved everything in, careful to cover the glaring mismatched nature of the items.

The comic book had a bright red superhero on the cover, which could pass as something Jack might like. The action figures were generic enough that they might not raise suspicion. And the baseball cap, well, who wouldn't like an extra hat, right?

Max took a step back, inspecting the bag. It didn't look great, but it was better than nothing. "He'll love it. It's… it's unique," Max said, trying to convince himself as much as anyone else.

When he arrived at Jack's birthday party, Max was greeted by a group of friends, all chatting and laughing. The smell of pizza and cake filled the air. Jack's mom smiled at him as she handed him a plate with a slice of cake, but Max couldn't help but feel a little guilty about the gift.

"Hey, Max! You made it!" Jack called from the living room. He looked excited as Max walked over, clutching the lopsided gift bag.

"Hey, Jack. Happy birthday!" Max said with a forced smile.

Jack grinned, "Thanks, man! I'm glad you're here. You didn't have to bring anything, though."

Max shrugged, still feeling nervous. "Nah, it's no big deal.

Just a little something for you." He handed over the bag, trying to make the whole thing seem casual.

Jack took the bag and pulled out the items one by one, his expression flickering with confusion.

"What's this?" Jack asked, holding up the baseball cap. "This is cool, but... I think it's a little too big for me."

Max laughed, trying to cover up his unease. "Yeah, I figured you could grow into it or use it for something else. You know, for style."

Jack's brow furrowed as he pulled out the comic book. "Uh... this is your comic book, Max. The one you borrowed from me last year."

Max stiffened, realizing his mistake. "Yeah, I figured I'd give it back as a gift. It's, uh, a rare edition. Super valuable! Trust me."

Jack looked at him, eyebrow raised. "Rare edition? Max, this is a regular comic book. It's not even in mint condition. And you gave me action figures... from like, every different series. What's going on here?"

Max felt the heat rise in his cheeks as his lie crumbled before him. "It's... uh, it's a limited edition collector's set," Max said weakly.

"I found it at a garage sale, really rare, you know?"

Jack just stared at him for a moment, then shook his head. "Max, I don't care about that. I care that you actually put thought into the gift. But this... this doesn't feel like something you put effort into. It feels like you just grabbed whatever you had lying around. And I'm not even sure you're being honest with me."

Max's stomach dropped. He had never seen Jack look so disappointed. The excitement from the party faded, and a cold sense of guilt settled over him.

"I... I'm sorry, Jack," Max mumbled, the words coming out reluctantly. "I didn't mean for it to look like I didn't care. I honestly just forgot about your birthday, and I didn't know what to get you. I'm sorry."

Jack blinked, a little surprised. "Wait, you forgot?"

Max sighed. "Yeah, I really messed up. I thought I could get away with it by giving you some stuff I already had. But I guess I should've just gotten you something nice and thought about it more."

Jack looked at him for a long moment before he gave a small smile. "It's okay, Max. Honestly, I'd rather have something real from you, not something you just threw together. I appreciate the effort, though."

Max nodded, feeling like a weight had been lifted from his shoulders. "Thanks for understanding, Jack."

But the whole situation weighed heavily on Max's mind as the party continued. He'd spent so much time avoiding the truth that now, it was all too clear: he had failed to put any real thought into Jack's gift. It wasn't just about the present; it was about the effort and care you put into the things you do for others.

As the day wore on, Max sat back and watched as Jack enjoyed the real gifts he had received. His friends laughed and joked, and for a brief moment, Max realized that Jack's joy didn't come from expensive presents or big gestures. It came from the thoughtfulness and effort people put into showing they cared.

Max knew what he had to do. It wasn't just about giving the right gift; it was about taking the time to show his friends he was there for them, that he valued them.

"I'll make it up to you, Jack. I promise," Max said quietly, as the two of them sat down to enjoy a slice of cake together.

Chapter 10: The Great Truth Reveal

Max's Excuse: "Okay, you caught me—no
excuses this time!"
Excuse Rating: 10/10 – Finally, the truth works!

Max sat on the edge of his bed, staring at his sneakers. The room was unusually quiet, and the weight of everything he had been hiding from his friends and family hung over him like a heavy cloud. He'd lied to cover up mistakes, avoid responsibility, and protect himself from the consequences of his actions. But as the days went by, the lies had only piled up, creating a tangled web that Max couldn't escape from.

He had learned the hard way: it was much easier to admit the truth from the beginning than it was to keep up with a series of excuses that never quite held up. And now, with Jack's birthday and the weird present debacle behind him, Max knew it was time to come clean.

He took a deep breath, then grabbed his phone. He typed out a message to his best friends: "Can we meet up? I need to talk."

The response was quick.

"Of course! Are you okay?" came the reply from Lila.

Max felt a pang of guilt. If only they knew the whole truth. But he couldn't avoid it any longer. He needed to face the consequences of his actions.

A few hours later, Max stood outside the local ice cream shop, waiting for his friends to arrive. The warm summer air wrapped around him, but his nerves made it feel cooler than it really was. He ran his fingers through his hair, trying to think of what he could say to make everything right.

Lila, Jack, and Emma appeared, their usual excitement about hanging out tempered with curiosity. They could tell something was off by the way Max was fidgeting.

"Hey, Max," Jack greeted him, looking concerned. "You said you needed to talk?"

Max nodded. "Yeah, I do. It's... it's a big deal."

They all sat down at the outdoor table, their ice cream cones forgotten for the moment as Max struggled to find the words. His friends waited patiently, their faces warm and understanding.

"I've been lying," Max started, his voice thick with guilt. "Not just to you guys, but to everyone. And it's gotten out of hand. I've lied to avoid getting in trouble, to skip out on responsibilities, and even to get out of doing stuff I didn't want to do."

His words hung in the air for a moment, and he could see the surprise and concern in their eyes.

They hadn't expected this, and Max could see them processing what he was saying.

"I lied about the pizza night," he continued, looking at each of their faces in turn. "I wasn't sick that night. I just didn't want to help. And I lied about the race too—I said my bike was sabotaged, but really, I just wasn't fast enough."

Lila reached out, her hand resting gently on his. "Max, we're your friends. You don't have to lie to us. We'd rather know the truth."

Max nodded, the knot in his stomach tightening. "I know. And I'm sorry. I've been so focused on avoiding consequences that I didn't think about how my lies were affecting you. I didn't think about how much harder it would be to keep all of this from you."

"Max," Jack said quietly, "We've been friends for a long time. We know you're not perfect, but we're not going to judge you for messing up. We just want the truth."

Max's chest felt lighter, and for the first time in what felt like forever, he could breathe without the constant worry of being caught in another lie. "I know I've messed up. And I know I've let you guys down. I've been hiding behind excuses, and it's made everything worse."

The relief in Max's voice was palpable, and his friends nodded in understanding.

"I've also been lying to my parents," Max admitted, feeling the weight of it all. "I told them I was doing better in school than I actually am. I told them I finished my chores, when I hadn't. I kept saying I was too busy for family stuff, but really, I was just avoiding things because I didn't want to admit I was struggling."

There was a long pause as his friends processed everything. Emma was the first to speak. "Max, it sounds like you've been really overwhelmed. But lying only made it harder for you, didn't it?"

Max nodded. "Yeah. It was like I kept digging myself into a deeper hole, and the more lies I told, the harder it was to climb out. And the worst part is, I've hurt the people I care about. I don't want to keep doing that."

Lila smiled softly. "It takes a lot of courage to admit the truth. We're glad you're telling us now." Max felt a rush of gratitude for his friends. It felt so good to be honest, even though it was hard. He had spent so much time trying to cover up his mistakes that he hadn't realized how much lighter he'd feel by simply being truthful.

"I promise I'll do better," Max said earnestly. "I don't want to keep lying to you guys. I want to be better, for myself and for all of you."

Jack gave him a playful shove. "You've got some making up to do, buddy. But we're with you."

Max's heart swelled with relief. It wasn't the end of his journey, but it felt like the beginning of something better. The truth had set him free from the web of lies he'd woven around himself. And while he knew there would be challenges ahead, he also knew that facing those challenges honestly was the way forward.

"I can't promise I won't mess up again," Max said with a sheepish grin. "But I'll always try to be honest with you."

"And that's all we ask," Lila replied with a smile.

As the group began to chat and laugh again, Max felt like a weight had been lifted from his shoulders. For the first time in a long while, he wasn't worried about what lies he might have to tell next. Instead, he could focus on enjoying the moment, knowing that he had finally told the truth.

Chapter 11: Truth Hurts, But It Heals

Max's Excuse: "Honesty feels... weird, but good!"
Excuse Rating: N/A – No excuses, just growth.

Max woke up to the soft glow of sunlight streaming through his window, feeling a sense of calm he hadn't experienced in a long time. His thoughts were no longer tangled in the web of lies he had spun over the past few months. For the first time, he felt free—free from the constant pressure of keeping his stories straight, free from the fear of being caught, and, most importantly, free from the guilt that had weighed him down.

As he got ready for school, Max couldn't help but smile at how much lighter everything felt. He'd come clean to his friends and family, and while it hadn't been easy, it had made things better. There was no more pretending. No more excuses. Just truth.

When he walked into the kitchen, his mom looked up from the breakfast table, her eyes filled with a gentle warmth. "How's my honest son doing this morning?" she teased.

Max chuckled, sitting down with a plate of pancakes. "Good," he said, his voice full of sincerity. "I feel good."

His mom smiled knowingly. "I'm proud of you, Max. It takes a lot of courage to be truthful, and I can see that you've learned something important."

Max's heart swelled with pride. He had apologized to his parents for the lies about his chores and schoolwork. They'd been disappointed, but they appreciated his honesty. And, for the first time, he didn't feel like he was hiding something from them.

At school, Max noticed the difference in how he interacted with his friends. He didn't have to think about what to say or how to cover up his mistakes. There was no weight on his shoulders. During lunch, Jack, Lila, and Emma sat together, and Max felt like their friendship had deepened.

"Hey, Max," Jack said, his eyes twinkling with mischief. "I heard you've become the 'truth-teller' around here."

Max grinned. "I guess I have. It's actually kind of nice."

Lila nudged him with a playful elbow. "You know, we could get you a trophy for your honesty. You could display it right next to your 'Master of Lies' award."

Max laughed. "I think I'd rather stick with the truth-telling trophy."

As the day went on, Max realized that honesty had a ripple effect.

His friendships felt more genuine, and he felt more connected to his classmates. He no longer had to worry about whether people would find out his secrets. The truth was out there, and it was okay.

Later that afternoon, Max's teacher, Mrs. Johnson, made an announcement. "Class, tomorrow we have a special assignment. Each of you will present your science project to the class. I want you to be as creative as possible and be honest about your work. Remember, it's not about being perfect—it's about trying your best and being true to what you've done."

Max's stomach dropped. He had completely forgotten about his science project. He hadn't even started it, and now he was expected to present it in front of the entire class. Panic set in as he tried to come up with a quick solution. He could tell another lie, claim he had technical difficulties, or make up some grand excuse about an experiment gone wrong. But as he stood there, his mind raced, he realized that wasn't the right choice anymore.

For the first time, Max decided to be honest.

He raised his hand and, when Mrs. Johnson called on him, said, "Actually, Mrs. Johnson, I haven't finished my project yet."

The class went quiet for a moment. Max felt his heart pounding in his chest, but he continued. "I know I was supposed to have it ready, but I didn't. And I'm sorry about that."

Mrs. Johnson smiled at him, her expression soft but serious. "Thank you for being honest, Max. That takes courage."

Max looked around the room. His classmates were staring at him, some with surprise, others with curiosity. But instead of judgment, he saw respect in their eyes. He wasn't sure how it had happened, but being truthful seemed to have earned him something far more valuable than a perfect project: respect.

The rest of the class went by quickly, and Max found himself feeling relieved, not because the day was over, but because he had told the truth and it hadn't been as hard as he thought. Sure, it wasn't the best situation—he had to stay up late working on the project—but being honest about it had made everything feel lighter.

When Max got home, he didn't try to avoid his parents or make up excuses.

He walked into the living room and sat down beside his mom. "I didn't finish my science project," he admitted again. "But I'll work on it tonight and make sure I do a good job."

His mom nodded approvingly. "I'm glad you're being responsible, Max. It's okay to make mistakes, but it's important to take ownership of them. And I'm proud of you for telling the truth."

That evening, Max sat down at his desk and worked on his science project. It wasn't perfect, but he didn't feel the pressure of lying anymore. He focused on doing his best, knowing that no matter the outcome, he had been honest. And that felt better than any lie ever could.

Chapter 12: Max's Magnificent Moment

Max's Excuse: "I didn't finish my project, but I'm working on it."
Excuse Rating: N/A – Honesty is my new superpower.

Max's palms were sweating, and his stomach felt like a knot of tangled string. He had never been more nervous in his life. His science project, or rather, the lack of it, stood in front of him. It wasn't finished. It wasn't even close to finished. But there it was, an unfinished experiment in a cluttered box, surrounded by a few hastily written notes and a couple of crumpled paper towels.

This was the moment. Max had two choices. He could lie. He could make up some excuse about how the experiment malfunctioned or how his pet hamster had eaten all the data sheets. He could pretend that everything was fine, that he had everything under control.

But he didn't. Not anymore. Not after all the lessons he had learned in the past few weeks. No, this time, Max was going to tell the truth.

"Uh, hi, everyone," Max started, his voice shaky. He looked out at his classmates, who were all staring at him, their eyes wide and curious. His teacher, Mrs. Johnson, sat at her desk, giving him a nod of encouragement. Max took a deep breath.

"I didn't finish my science project," he admitted, feeling a weight lift off his shoulders with each word.

"I know I was supposed to have it done, but I didn't. And I'm really sorry about that."

The room went quiet. Max could feel his heart pounding in his chest. He waited for someone to laugh, for someone to mock him for being so honest. But it never came. Instead, Mrs. Johnson stood up and smiled warmly at him.

"Thank you for being honest, Max," she said. "It's not always easy to admit when we're behind or when things don't go as planned. But the truth is always a good place to start."

Max swallowed hard, his nerves still rattling, but now there was a small spark of relief. He glanced around the room. Some of his classmates looked surprised, but they didn't look angry or disappointed. In fact, he could swear he saw a couple of them nodding in agreement. They'd probably been in the same situation before, too.

"I know it's not what I was supposed to present, but I can tell you what I've learned so far," Max continued, trying to steady his voice. "I was working on a project about chemical reactions, but I didn't have enough time to finish it. I got caught up with schoolwork and stuff at home. But I want to show you what I've done.

The experiment is supposed to show how vinegar and baking soda react, and—well, this is what happens."

Max dropped a spoonful of baking soda into a glass jar filled with vinegar. The fizzy reaction was immediate, and a cloud of bubbles rushed up the sides of the jar. It wasn't a grand spectacle, but it was something. A simple experiment, but a true one.

"That's it," Max said. "It's not much, but it works. And I promise to finish the rest of the project. I just didn't get around to it in time."

Mrs. Johnson's smile widened, and she clapped her hands lightly. "Well done, Max. You've demonstrated the most important part of this experiment: learning. You're being honest with yourself and with us, and that's something we all can appreciate."

Max's classmates nodded in agreement, and some of them even smiled back at him. He hadn't expected this. He thought they would all be disappointed in him, but instead, they seemed...understanding.

Even Emma, who was usually quick to point out anyone's mistakes, gave him an encouraging thumbs-up.

"Thank you, Max," Mrs. Johnson said. "It's clear that you've learned something today, and that's what matters. Honesty might not always be the easiest option, but it's the right one. I'm proud of you for standing up here and sharing the truth with us."

Max felt a rush of pride swell in his chest. He wasn't the best in the class. His project wasn't the most creative or complex. But he had done the right thing. He had been truthful. And that was all that mattered.

The rest of the class went by in a blur. As each student presented their project, Max sat back, reflecting on how far he had come. He wasn't just presenting a science project anymore; he was presenting the new version of himself. A version who no longer hid behind lies. A version who was ready to face the world, mistakes and all.

As the bell rang, signaling the end of the school day, Max packed up his things. His classmates filed out, some chatting with him about their projects, others giving him small nods of acknowledgment. He felt like he had earned something—respect, perhaps.

Or maybe it was just the peace of knowing he no longer had to carry the burden of pretending.

When Max walked into the hallway, he spotted his mom waiting for him outside the classroom. She had that look on her face, the one that told Max she was proud of him, but she didn't need to say anything. He had already figured it out.

"Hey, Mom," Max said, giving her a smile. "You won't believe what happened in class today."

She raised an eyebrow, curious. "Tell me."

"I told the truth," Max said, his grin wide. "And it felt amazing."

His mom laughed softly, brushing a stray lock of hair from his face. "I'm glad to hear that. You've learned something important, Max. Truth is always the best option, even if it's hard sometimes."

"I know," Max replied. "And from now on, I'm going to stick with the truth. It's way less stressful than trying to keep track of all those lies."

As they walked down the hall, Max felt a lightness in his chest.

He had faced his fear of being honest, and in return, he had earned something far more valuable than any lie could provide: respect, peace, and a future built on the truth.

Chapter 13: The Excuse-Free Future

Max stood in front of the mirror, his reflection staring back at him. He adjusted the collar of his shirt, a small habit he'd picked up recently whenever he felt nervous—or in this case, proud. It wasn't a big moment like a birthday or an award ceremony, but it was a significant one. He had made it. Max was no longer the kid who scrambled for excuses to cover up his mistakes. He wasn't the one who hid behind lies to avoid responsibility. He was different now.

His room was quiet, except for the soft ticking of the clock on the wall. The same clock that had always been there, marking time as it passed. But today, Max didn't feel like time was rushing past him. He felt like he was in control of it for the first time in a long while.

The lessons he had learned over the past few weeks had changed him. They had peeled away layers of fear and self-doubt, revealing someone he hadn't fully recognized before. Someone stronger. More honest. Someone ready to face the world, no matter what it threw his way.

He ran his fingers through his hair, taking a deep breath. The future wasn't something he used to think about much.

It was always easier to think in the present—making excuses for why things didn't go well, brushing off problems, and pretending they weren't there. But now, Max had learned that running from problems didn't solve them. They only grew bigger.

Max turned around and looked at his bed, where his backpack sat neatly packed. It was ready for the next day at school, another day full of possibilities. He knew there would still be challenges ahead. There would be moments when it was tempting to slip back into old habits —when a lie would seem like an easy way out, when making excuses might feel like the simpler option. But Max had something now that he didn't have before: the confidence that the truth was always the better path.

The knock on his door broke his thoughts. His mom peeked her head around the corner, her smile warm and reassuring. "You ready for dinner?" she asked.

Max nodded. "Yeah. I'm ready."

"Good," she said, stepping inside. "I'm proud of you, you know that?"

Max blinked, surprised by the sudden rush of emotion he felt. "Thanks, Mom.

I've been thinking a lot about... about everything."

"About the truth?" she asked, sitting on the edge of his bed.

Max nodded again, his voice steady now. "Yeah. I'm done with excuses. I don't want to hide anymore. I don't want to be afraid of facing what's real. I want to be someone who can be proud of what I say and do."

His mom's smile widened, and she pulled him into a quick hug. "I'm proud of you, too, Max. More than you know."

As they walked down the stairs together, Max couldn't help but reflect on how far he had come. He had started out as the kid who couldn't tell the truth without getting caught. The one who tried to make excuses when things went wrong. But now, as he entered the kitchen, where his dad was setting the table, Max saw everything in a new light.

His dad looked up from his work and gave him an approving nod. "How's the school project going, Max?"

"It's all done," Max replied confidently. "And I presented it honestly, even though it wasn't perfect. I told them the truth, and Mrs. Johnson appreciated it."

"That's great, son. Keep that attitude. Honesty is more important than being perfect."

Max smiled. He had heard those words many times before, but now they meant something different. He didn't need to be perfect. He didn't need to have everything figured out. What mattered was that he was trying, and that he was being honest with himself and others.

That was enough.

Dinner was filled with laughter and light conversation. Max noticed how much easier it was to talk now that he didn't have to hide behind any lies or excuses. It felt good to be open, to let people see him for who he truly was. His friends at school had started to treat him differently, too. They respected him more now, not because he was always right or had the best answers, but because they knew he could be trusted.

As the evening wore on and his family gathered together, Max's thoughts turned to the future. He knew that life wouldn't always be easy. He would face setbacks, disappointments, and moments of doubt. But now, he had a new perspective.

He had learned that being honest with himself and others wasn't just about telling the truth— it was about owning his choices, taking responsibility, and trusting that the truth would guide him through anything.

The future didn't seem as scary anymore. It was full of possibilities. New challenges awaited, but Max was no longer afraid to face them. He wasn't afraid of failure. He wasn't afraid of making mistakes. Because he knew that as long as he was truthful, everything else would fall into place.

Max stood up from the table and walked over to the window, looking out into the darkening sky. The stars twinkled brightly overhead, and for the first time, he felt like he was part of something bigger. Something true.

The End

Maxed Out on Excuses TikTok Challenge

Ready to Max-out your excuses? Join the MaxedOutOnExcuses challenge and show off your wildest, funniest, and most outrageous excuses—just like Max! It's your chance to get creative, have a blast, and dodge responsibilities in the most hilarious ways possible!

How to Join the Challenge:

1. Dream Up Your Best Excuse: Think of an over-the-top excuse for anything—whether it's why you didn't do your homework, why you're late to class, or why you absolutely can't take out the trash today. Make it wild, funny, and completely out of this world!

2. Act It Out: Use props, dramatic acting, and your wild imagination to bring your excuse to life. Is it aliens? A mischievous hamster? A magical snowstorm? The sky's the limit!

3. Create Your TikTok: Film your excuse in a fun TikTok video. The more ridiculous and over-the-top, the better! Feel free to add in funny sound effects, special effects, or even a costume to make it even more epic.

4. Tag and Share: Post your video and make sure to use the hashtag **#MaxedOutOnExcuses** in your caption so Max can find your hilarious excuses! Tag a few friends to get them in on the challenge too, and spread the laugh!

Disclaimer: No actual excuses will be accepted in real life. Max says the truth is always the best answer—except for on TikTok!

A Note from Max

Hey there, future excuse-making champions!

So, here's the deal: I've learned a lot on this wild ride of excuses and truths, and I want to share a little secret with you. Sure, coming up with crazy excuses can be fun and all, but nothing beats the freedom of telling the truth. (Trust me, I've learned the hard way!)

The best part? You have a superpower—your imagination! It's like a secret weapon that can take you on the coolest adventures, solve tricky problems, and come up with the funniest ideas. Just remember: it's okay to make mistakes. We all do it, and that's how we grow. It's not about being perfect, it's about owning up, learning, and having fun while you do it.

So, whether you're facing a tricky situation, a tough challenge, or a science project (ugh!), remember this: your creativity and honesty will get you through anything. Keep dreaming big, telling your story, and laughing at all the wild things life throws your way.

Go out there, be awesome, and don't forget to have a little fun!

Your pal,
Max

Made in the USA
Las Vegas, NV
01 February 2025

17367121R00049